~ BEDROOMS ~

BEDROOMS

Jessica Elin Hirschman

MetroBooks

DEDICATION

For my twin sister, Jennifer Elin, in fond recollection of the bedrooms
we shared throughout the years.

ACKNOWLEDGMENTS

Furniture designer and consummate historian Steven Hodges deserves special thanks for his
enthusiastic and thorough research assistance. Thanks also goes to the Better Sleep Council, to
the talented staff at the Michael Friedman Publishing Group, and to the designers and home
owners who graciously allowed me into their very private worlds.

MetroBooks

An Imprint of the Michael Friedman Publishing Group, Inc.

First MetroBooks edition 2003

©1996 by Michael Friedman Publishing Group, Inc.

Library of Congress Cataloging-in-Publication Data available upon request.

ISBN 1-58663-791-6

Editor: Kelly Matthews
Art Director: Jeff Batzli
Designer: Lynne Yeamans
Photography Editor: Christopher C. Bain
Production Manager: Karen Matsu Greenberg

Color separations by Bright Arts (Singapore) Pte. Ltd.
Printed in China by C.S. Graphics Shanghai

1 3 5 7 9 10 8 6 4 2

For bulk purchases and special sales, please contact:
Michael Friedman Publishing Group, Inc.
Attention: Sales Department
230 Fifth Avenue
New York, NY 10001
212/685-6610   FAX 212/685-3916

Visit our website:
www.metrobooks.com

TABLE OF CONTENTS

INTRODUCTION ▣ 6

PART ONE: BEDROOM ANATOMY ▣ 10

PART TWO: PERSONAL TOUCHES ▣ 50

SOURCES ▣ 70

INDEX ▣ 72

INTRODUCTION

Be it through myth or lore, tradition or ritual, history has grandly bestowed attention upon the bed and, by extension, the bedroom. The evolution of bed and bedroom design encompasses the history of science, art, and philosophy. Refinements in the look and feel of beds — and bedrooms — reflect advancements in technology, achievements in art, and changes in life-styles.

From its basic utilitarian beginnings, the bed has been the focal point of design development in the bedroom. Historical documents reveal that ancient Egyptian, Greek, and Roman peoples slept on well-formed bed structures. They draped animal skins and soft textiles over wood, stone, or metal frames to enhance comfort. Persian nomads slept on water-filled goatskins for the same purpose. The wealthy members of these societies decorated their beds with metal, ivory, wood carvings, and jewels to designate their privileged positions.

Such handiwork also reflected the particular significance of art and philosophy in ancient cultures. Egyptian pharaohs, who spent their mortal lives accumulating wealth and possessions for the afterlife, were entombed with several stately beds to sustain them through their postmortem journeys. Roman emperors decorated their beds and sleeping chambers with inlaid gold and carvings of animals that symbolized strength. These practices established the bed as both a design statement and a symbol of personal stature.

Bed height and embellishments such as canopies and drapes were also signs of wealth and privilege. For example, some Swedish farming cultures and European nobility shared a belief that the higher the bed stood off the floor the more successful and prosperous the family was and would continue to be. Similarly, bed size was also indicative of personal and familial stature. Until the eighteenth century, when room design and furniture became simpler and scaled down, bigger signified richer. In Queen Anne England, beds measuring seven by eight feet (2.1 by 2.4m) and eleven feet (3.3m) high were popular among those who could afford their high price tags. Layers of luxurious fabrics — satin, silks, velvets, gold-embroidered tapestries — draped canopies that soared as high as sixteen feet (4.8m).

Left: THE CASUAL CHARM OF THIS RESTFUL BEDROOM REFLECTS THE OWNER'S RELAXED LIFE-STYLE AND ECLECTIC DESIGN SENSIBILITIES. THE HERRINGBONE COTTON CANOPY IS DRAPED EFFORTLESSLY OVER A SUSPENDED POLE AND BALANCED BY A COUNTERWEIGHT, ECHOING THE ARCHITECTURAL DETAILS.

William Shakespeare immortalized one of history's most infamous colossal beds in his play *Twelfth Night*. The appropriately named "Great Bed of Ware," located at the Inn of Ware in England, measured twelve feet (3.6m) square and reportedly accommodated as many as sixty-eight guests at one time.

Perhaps the only period during which opulent beds and lavish bedrooms fell from favor was the Middle Ages. During this austere time, nobility and civilian alike slept on straw-filled sacks in fortresslike rooms. The emphasis was on personal survival rather than creature comforts. In fact, it wasn't until the sixteenth century that beds became somewhat permanent and warranted superfluous splendor.

Prior to that time, beds were disassembled, packed, and carried from residence to residence. Even draperies were boxed and transported to the new bedroom. (Reportedly, the practice of surrounding the bed with a curtain began during the Crusades.) As extravagant as some of these curtains were, they served the practical function of enclosing the bed for desired privacy.

In the sixteenth century, the advent of corner posts heralded a great change in bed design and bedroom decor. Beds were no longer collapsible. Four-poster designs eventually gave way to two-poster beds with heavy, intricately carved headboards adding even more prominence — and a permanent feel — to the bed and bedroom. These beds were more than de rigueur; Tudor headboards often brandished the occupant's coat of arms and other elaborate designs.

Exaggerated beds were just as popular in fourteenth-, fifteenth-, and sixteenth-century France, where the revival of art and style flourished throughout the Renaissance. Beds were constructed with as many as thirty textile parts and virtually no visible wood. Voluminous drapes, plumes, and fringed valances adorned state beds. After centuries of such opulence, however, eighteenth-century furniture design witnessed a dramatic change in the shape and construction of the bed.

English cabinetmaker Thomas Sheraton spearheaded a scaling back of proportions. Beds — and other furniture — became lighter and more refined. Simplicity replaced complexity. During this period, beds designed by such preeminent craftsmen as Chippendale, Hepplewhite, and Adams remained decorative but were smaller in scale. Materials also took on a lighter, more airy look as iron and brass-tubing frames came into favor around the middle of the century. Beds from this time and the

subsequent Empire period are still the primary models for many modern-day designs.

The *lit en bateau* — French for boat bed — was a particularly popular style. With high straight-backed ends, the design resembled a boat and inspired one of the most enduring of all bed styles, the sleigh bed. Introduced more than one hundred and fifty years ago, the American Empire sleigh bed was carved primarily from mahogany and featured matching scrolled headboards and footboards connected by low wood side rails. Its wood framing was reminiscent of a sleigh and was especially well suited for supporting the laced-rope mattresses of nineteenth-century beds. Whether traditional or interpretive, the shape of today's sleigh beds remains fairly true to form: blocky, low to the ground, and undraped.

In many ways, the history of the bed is the history of the bedroom. But as colorful as this heritage may be, it is not the whole story. Bedrooms are more than just display cases for ornate beds. They are the public expression of the most private self, a record of how each occupant chooses to live, relax, and partake in the cycle of life.

The photographs presented in this book were selected for their power to entice — and to revive the design and enjoyment of bedrooms. Approach this book not only as a captivating glance into sacrosanct, private worlds but also as a time capsule preserving the tradition of fine bedroom design.

Above: A SUBSTANTIAL CANOPY AND VOLUMINOUS DRAPES CREATE AN INTIMATE SETTING FOR A BED IN THIS UNUSUALLY LARGE ROOM. THE SAME HEAVY CANVAS FABRIC COVERS THE WALLS, AN EFFECT THAT VISUALLY SOOTHES AND ACOUSTICALLY QUIETS THE SPACE. BEYOND, THE FORMER SLEEPING PORCH SERVES AS AN ADJACENT SITTING AREA.

Part One: Bedroom Anatomy

Bedrooms are such wonderful places. To an adult, a bedroom is the private oasis that guards the soul, rekindles the spirit, and provides a sanctuary for tender abandon. To a young child, a bedroom is at once a playground, classroom, art studio, and keeper of all dreams. And bridging the bedrooms of childhood and adulthood is the sanctuary of adolescence, that very personal haven where every teenager seeks answers to—and refuge from—the mysteries of growing up.

Because bedrooms fulfill such a variety of emotional, psychological, and physical needs, their design must incorporate and reconcile numerous elements. They should be appealing to the eye as well as the mind, as beautiful as they are functional. Architecture, lighting, storage, flooring, wall treatments, and bedding ensembles—to name a few concerns—must all be considered

in addition to the most fundamental element: the selection and placement of the bed.

It's been said that the position of a bed within a room says something about the habits and life-style of the occupant, specifically how he or she likes to begin and end each day. The Oriental philosophy of Feng Shui goes even further, relating the position of the bed to overall health and well-being. The principles of Feng Shui, as applied to the bedroom, hold that a badly placed bed will lead to restless nights.

Since the bed is usually the focal point of the bedroom, it often dictates how the balance of the room is furnished and used. Still, the bed need not be the overriding influence in bedroom design and decor, as evidenced by the following pictures. Personal tastes, individual life-styles, and even heritage often influence the look and feel of a bedroom.

Left: THE SENSE OF SAFETY AND ENCLOSURE IN THIS ROOM IS HEIGHTENED BY INTENSE RED LACQUER ON THE WALLS AND CEILING. THE WOOD BOX-STYLE BED FRAME BORROWS ELEMENTS FROM GREEK TEMPLE DESIGN. **Above:** A SOPHISTICATED, SIMPLE BALANCE OF COLOR AND PATTERN ACCENTED BY ANTIQUE WALLPAPER GIVES THIS URBAN BEDROOM A TIMELESS APPEARANCE BY DAY AND A RESTFUL, COZY GLOW BY NIGHT.

Above: USING THE SAME TEXTILE FOR ALL UPHOLSTERY AND FABRIC APPLICATIONS IS PARTICULARLY SUCCESSFUL IN A SMALL SPACE WHERE MULTIPLE COLORS OR PATTERNS COULD APPEAR OVERWHELMING. HERE, AN ELEGANT MAHOGANY BED FRAME AND MATCHING CROWN MOLDING RESTRAIN AN EXUBERANT ENGLISH CHINTZ. **Right:** IN THE EARLY 1700S, SOME TESTERS (CANOPIES) AND BED DRAPES MEASURED AS HIGH AS SIXTEEN FEET (4.8M). IN THOSE DAYS, THE SIZE OF FULL-LENGTH TESTERS AND LONG, HEAVY DRAPES REFLECTED THE WEALTH AND STATUS OF THE OCCUPANT. THIS PROMINENT BEDROOM IS FURNISHED IN ANGLO-INDIAN STYLE. THE CANOPY AND DRAPES ARE A TRADITIONAL INDIAN *IKAT* FABRIC; THE CONVERSATION AREA FEATURES A CUSTOM *RAJ*-STYLE TEA TABLE AND A VICTORIAN-STYLE LOVE SEAT. AN ORIGINAL NINETEENTH-CENTURY CARTOON WALL HANGING AND SILK MOIRÉ WALLPAPER FILL THE FAR WALL; SILVER LEAF PAPER ON THE CEILING CASTS AN ELEGANT SHIMMER ACROSS THE ROOM.

Left: EVERY ELEMENT OF THIS CONTEMPORARY BEDROOM IS DESIGNED TO TAKE ADVANTAGE OF THE BEAUTIFUL LANDSCAPE BEYOND, WHICH INCLUDES A SMALL-SCALE MAN-MADE LAKE. LOCATING THE BED AT AN ANGLE BENEATH AN INTENTION-ALLY SKEWED SKYLIGHT AFFORDS A DRAMATIC VIEW AT SUNRISE AND SUNSET. JUXTAPOSING PRISTINELY FINISHED INTERIORS WITH AN EXPOSED CEILING CREATES THE ARCHITECTURAL ILLUSION OF A SPACE WITHIN A SPACE.

Left: USUALLY THE FOCAL POINT OF A BEDROOM, THE BED IN THIS SETTING RESTS LOW TO THE GROUND SO AS NOT TO COMPETE WITH THE DESIGN OF THE SPACE. A SIMPLE PATCHWORK QUILT PROVIDES THE BED WITH A SUBTLE PROMINENCE BENEATH THE HAND-PAINTED WALL. THE PASTEL COLOR SCHEME VISUALLY SOFTENS THE CONCRETE, WOOD, AND GLASS SURFACES.

Left: THIS *LIT EN BALDAQUIN*—A CANOPIED BED PLACED FLUSH AGAINST THE WALL TO FUNCTION AS A COUCH—IS DRESSED IN THE SAME HAUNTING SHADES OF BLUE AND GREEN THAT ENVELOP THE TINY ROOM. THE INTENSE COLORS, SET OFF BY THE RICH-TONED WOOD BED FRAME AND BRASS CANDLESTICKS, ADD DRAMA AND MYSTERY TO THE SPACE. SOME PEOPLE BELIEVE THE COLOR BLUE ENHANCES THE ABILITY TO REMEMBER DREAMS.

Above: IN AN IRISH CASTLE, SHADES OF DEEP BLUE HEIGHTEN THE CONTRAST BETWEEN THE RICH YELLOW WALLS AND VIVIDLY PATTERNED SHEETS. A REGAL BLUE DAMASK ADORNS THE CHAIRS. **Left:** MEXICAN ARCHITECT MARCO ALDACO ONCE EXPRESSED THE BELIEF THAT PEOPLE ARE MORE TRANQUIL IN ROOMS WITH CURVES. THE GENTLY CURVED BLUE WALLS OF THIS 1896 BEDROOM EVOKE A FEELING OF INFINITE PEACE AND QUIET.

Above: AT THE END OF A BUSY DAY, THE OCCUPANT OF THIS SUBDUED BEDROOM FINDS TRUE REPOSE FROM HER WORK IN THE VISUAL WORLD. THE MONOCHROMATIC COLOR SCHEME AND ABSENCE OF ARTWORK, SAVE FOR THE ILLUMINATED STARBURST, HELP CALM THE ROOM. **Right:** HAWAIIAN FABRICS TURN THE BEDROOM OF A 1950S CALIFORNIA BUNGALOW INTO A LUSH TROPICAL RETREAT. CURTAINS SEWN FROM *PAREO* CLOTH, WHICH IS TYPICALLY WORN AS CLOTHING, FRAME A BAMBOO BUREAU.

Left: Traditionally, Japanese futons are brought out only at night and placed atop tatamis—straw mats that provide a basic floor covering and some insulation. By day, the futons are rolled and stored out of sight. In this peaceful bedroom, the boulder and rock vase represent the importance of nature in Oriental philosophies and life-styles.

Left: A tatami bed stands serenely among minimal appointments in this New Delhi bedroom designed to honor the Buddhist tradition of living among sparse surroundings that are conducive to contemplation. Right: Although thoroughly modern, this London bedroom bears the distinctive hallmark of centuries-old Oriental design: purity of form and function.

Right: WHEN THE WORLD OF FANTASY MEETS THE VISION OF A TALENTED SET DESIGNER, THE RESULT IS AN INDULGENT, MAGICAL BEDROOM FROM ANOTHER TIME AND PLACE. ON ONE DEEP RED WALL, A CURIOUS COLLECTION OF BRIC-A-BRAC AND POSTCARDS CREATES THE ILLUSION OF A FARAWAY SPACE AWASH IN INTRIGUE AND ROMANCE. **Far right:** CROSSING THE THRESHOLD OF THIS VISUAL EXTRAVAGANZA IS LIKE STEPPING REVERENTLY INTO AN INDIAN PALACE OVERFLOWING WITH SILKEN OPULENCE. ACTUALLY, THE SHIMMERING FABRICS ARE INEXPENSIVE TEXTILES FROM THE DESIGNER-OWNER'S FAVORITE HAUNT: HOLLYWOOD BOULEVARD.

Above: A RESTORED, SPOOL-TURNED BED IS A FITTING CENTERPIECE IN A BEDROOM TUCKED UNDER THE EAVES OF A ROCKY MOUNTAIN LOG CABIN. A FEW CAREFULLY DISPLAYED PIECES OF CHINA PAY QUIET TRIBUTE TO THE FAMILY'S NEW ENGLAND ROOTS.

Right: AUTHENTIC FURNISHINGS PERSONALIZE THE BEDROOM OF AN AVID COLLECTOR OF WESTERN MEMORABILIA. HIGHLIGHTS INCLUDE A GENUINE 1930 MEXICAN SERAPE OVER THE PILLOWS, A MONTEREY BED FRAME, AND A CORONADO TABLE (TO THE LEFT OF THE BED). THE OCCUPANT ASSEMBLED THE LAMP FROM A CAST-OFF SHADE AND REAL STIRRUP.

Left: Nestling a bedroom, storage space, and adjacent bathroom into a small prewar Manhattan brownstone—with only one window—requires a lot of ingenuity. Here, glass blocks conceal the bathroom and illuminate the mezzanine-level bedroom. Cantilevered stairs appear to float along the wall, enhancing the room's feeling of openness.

Below: An improvised bunk bed assembled from painted industrial shelving serves as desk, dining table, china cabinet, and home office.

Left: This postmodern bedroom suite could easily pass for a spacious studio apartment. It's the top floor of a renovated urban warehouse. A custom-designed media center divides the space physically and visually. The "power tower," constructed from burled laminate with fuchsia accents, hides lighting and stereo equipment. The television swivels for easy viewing from either side. The same burled laminate finish is applied to the bed and custom-made combination headboard-desk.

Above: A REVERSIBLE EGYPTIAN COTTON DAMASK SWAGGED SYMMETRICALLY BEHIND A CUSTOM-DESIGNED BED TURNS A SIZABLE BEDROOM INTO A ROMANTIC BEDOUIN TENT. THE BED, MADE FROM POLISHED WHITE ASH WITH AN IVORY FINISH, FEATURES MINIATURE TURRETLIKE FINIALS ON ALL FOUR POSTS TO COMPLETE THE ROOM'S MOORISH LOOK. **Right:** APPROXIMATELY FOUR HUNDRED YARDS (365.7M) OF FRENCH PROVINCIAL PRINTED COTTON DISGUISES THE MODERN STREAMLINED ARCHITECTURE OF THIS GUEST BEDROOM. THE BED IS AN ORIGINAL LOUIS XVI PIECE, THE CHANDELIER ITALIAN, AND THE NEEDLEWORK RUG PORTUGUESE.

Left: FOUR-POSTER BEDS BECAME POPULAR IN THE EARLY SIXTEENTH CENTURY AND HAVE BEEN AT HOME IN THE BEDROOM EVER SINCE. HERE, A TRADITIONAL PENCIL-POST BED AND HAND-SEWN QUILT CAPTURE THE RESTRAINED BEAUTY AND TIMELESS APPEAL OF SHAKER FURNISHINGS. **Above, left:** RESTORING AN AUTHENTIC AMBIANCE OFTEN CALLS FOR A BALANCE OF NEW AND OLD. HERE, IN AN 1819 FEDERAL PERIOD HOME, THE CUSTOM-DESIGNED FLAT WOVEN RAG WOOL RUG IS NEW BUT THE REVERSIBLE JACQUARD BEDSPREAD, TRIMMED WITH A PATTERN CALLED OLD BOSTON TOWN, IS GENERATIONS OLD. **Above, right:** THE HOMESPUN JACQUARD COVERLET DRAPING THIS BED DATES FROM THE SAME PERIOD AS THE STONE FARMHOUSE. THE FURNISHINGS, INCLUDING A 1790 CHERRY LINEN PRESS AND HANDCRAFTED CHAIRS, ARE TYPICAL OF THE EIGHTEENTH CENTURY.

Right: TO MAXIMIZE THE LIMITED FLOOR SPACE OF THIS SHARED CHILDREN'S BEDROOM, THE ARCHITECT CREATED A VERTICAL, MULTIPURPOSE BED SYSTEM WITH AMPLE ROOM FOR STORAGE AND DIFFERENT LEVELS FOR CLIMBING. STACKING THE BEDS IN THIS MANNER LEFT ROOM ENOUGH FOR A PLAYHOUSE AND CREATED A CONTINUOUS CANVAS FOR DECORATIVE PAINTING.

Left: CHILDREN NEED LOTS OF ROOM FOR CREATIVITY. THIS HIDEAWAY DESK AND PULLOUT AQUARIUM ENCOURAGE NEAT PARTICIPATION IN THE ARTS AND SCIENCES OF GROWING UP. POCKET DOORS CONCEAL THE BOOKCASE AND DESK WHEN NOT IN USE.

Right: THE UGLY DUCKLING, RUMPELSTILTSKIN, THE FROG PRINCE, AND OTHER CHERISHED FAIRY TALES COME TOGETHER IN THIS CHILD'S ROOM. THE MIXED-MEDIA MURAL WAS WORKED ON CANVAS THAT WAS STRETCHED AND SIZED TO COVER THE WALL. THIS METHOD, RATHER THAN PAINTING DIRECTLY ONTO THE WALL SURFACE, ALLOWS THE HOME OWNER TO CHANGE THE SCENE AS THE CHILD GROWS UP.

Left: KING ARTHUR'S FABLED KNIGHTS OF THE ROUND TABLE LIVE ON IN A YOUNG BOY'S ROOM FINISHED WITH A HAND-PAINTED SCENE OF MEDIEVAL ENCHANTMENT. ELEGANT FABRICS AND REGAL COLORS ADD TO THE MAGIC OF THE IMAGINARY CASTLE HIDEAWAY. TROMPE L'OEIL MURALS ARE AN ARTFUL ALTERNATIVE TO ORDINARY PAINT OR WALLPAPER WHEN IT COMES TO DECORATING AND PERSONALIZING A CHILD'S BEDROOM.

Right, above: DECIDEDLY CONTEMPORARY AND CLASSICALLY ELEGANT, THE FOCAL POINT OF THIS APARTMENT BEDROOM IS THE EXAGGERATED METAL SLEIGH BED SHOWCASED ALONGSIDE AN ARTISTIC ROOM DIVIDER. **Right, below:** AN ARCHITECT'S OWN WHIMSICAL BEDROOM REPRESENTS A PEACEFUL SETTING AMONG THE FRAGRANT CALIFORNIA ORANGE GROVES. MAJESTIC MOUNTAINS ON THE HEADBOARD AND AN ARCHED REDWOOD CEILING SUGGESTING A SUNSET-COLORED SKY COMPLETE THE FANTASY LANDSCAPE. **Far right:** MORE REMINISCENT OF AN ART GALLERY THAN A BEDROOM, THIS CONTOURED ROOM EXHIBITS RARE ARCHITECTURAL PRINTS, ORIGINAL ARTWORK BY THE OCCUPANT'S FRIENDS, AND A WIDE-ANGLE VIEW OF NATURE'S OWN HANDIWORK. THE CONVERTED HOSPITAL TROLLEY IS ITSELF A PIECE OF UNCONVENTIONAL ART.

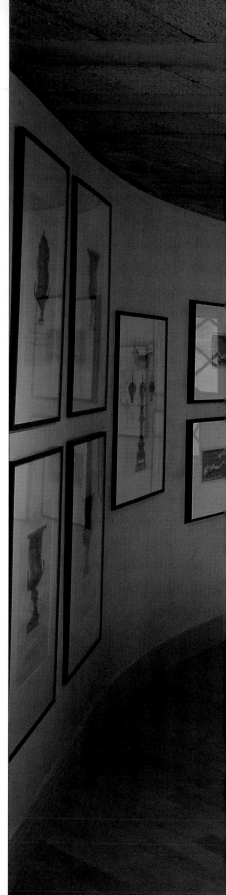

Right: THE REMODELED ATTIC OF A VICTORIAN HOME WAS OPENED TO THE OUTSIDE WITH A CUSTOM-MADE SKYLIGHT AND BALCONY ADDITION. AN ORIGINAL ARTS AND CRAFTS WINDOW ABOVE THE BED, NATURAL WOOD ACCENTS, AND OAK FLOORING PRESERVE THE OLD-FASHIONED SPIRIT OF THE NEWLY RENOVATED SPACE. **Below:** THE ABILITY TO MOVE FREELY BETWEEN AN INTIMATE, SHELTERED SPACE TO ONE THAT IS UNPROTECTED AND PUBLIC IS A TRUE LUXURY. THE FRENCH DOORS LEADING TO THIS SECOND-STORY DECK OPEN OUT, RATHER THAN IN, TO EMPHASIZE THE FEELING OF UNINTERRUPTED SPACE BETWEEN THE MASTER BEDROOM AND THE OUTSIDE. THE DECK ALSO MAXIMIZES THE BENEFITS OF A YEAR-ROUND WARM CLIMATE.

Right: PERHAPS ONE OF THE MOST ROMANTIC, ENVIABLE ATTRIBUTES OF ANY BEDROOM IS A BALCONY. THE MAHOGANY-BALUSTERED BALCONY OFF THIS BEDROOM IN A SEVENTEENTH-CENTURY HOME IN THE ANCIENT WALLED CITY OF CARTAGENA, COLOMBIA, OVERLOOKS AN INNER COURTYARD AND FOUNTAIN. THE ROOM ITSELF STILL HAS THE ORIGINAL 1593 BRICK FLOOR AND TROPICAL HARDWOOD CEILING BEAMS, WHICH SUPPORT THE FLOOR OF THE ROOM ABOVE.

Above: EXPANSES OF GLASS ARE POPULAR ARCHITECTURAL METHODS FOR VISUALLY OPENING UP A ROOM. CENTERED AMONG SYMMETRICAL BLOCKS OF MEXICAN GLASS, A FIREPLACE INTRODUCES A SECOND KIND OF NATURAL WARMTH AND LIGHT TO THIS CONTEMPORARY BEDROOM. THE EYE-CATCHING MATERIAL ON THE FLOOR AND CEILING IS ORIENTED STRAND BOARD THAT HAS BEEN FINISHED WITH A URETHANE VARNISH. **Left:** FLOOR-TO-CEILING GLASS CAN CHANGE THE ENTIRE MOOD OF A ROOM AS LIGHT AND SHADOWS INTERACT UNPREDICTABLY THROUGHOUT THE DAY. HERE, AN INTERPRETIVE PINE CANOPY HANGS FROM THIN STAINLESS STEEL WIRES DESIGNED TO GRACEFULLY REFLECT INCOMING SUNSHINE AND MOONLIGHT. GAZING THROUGH THE OVERHEAD STRUCTURE AT NIGHT GIVES THE ILLUSION OF STARING INTO A DEEP BLUE, SPARKLING SKY.

Right: THE ONLY THING MISSING FROM THIS SPACIOUS MASTER BEDROOM WAS A DRESSING AREA THAT WOULD PROVIDE CONSIDERABLE STORAGE WITHOUT BEING TOO INTRUSIVE. THE SOLUTION: A STEPPED STORAGE UNIT BUILT IN FRONT OF THE WALL CLOSETS. THE DESIGN ADDS UNEXPECTED DIMENSION TO THE ROOM'S MODERN ARCHITECTURE, AND THE MOLDING TRIM IS REPEATED THROUGHOUT THE HOUSE.

Left: FROM THE OTHER SIDE, THE ADJUSTABLE CUBBIES PROVIDE OPEN STORAGE FOR THE HOMEOWNER'S COLLECTION OF SHIRTS AND SWEATERS AND FORM A SEMIPRIVATE DRESSING SPACE.

Below: This contemporary urban home is designed on a grid. Various structural and design elements echo that plan throughout the house. In the second-story bedroom, a gridded screen partially separates the bed and dressing areas. The interlocking structure was fabricated from painted fir and galvanized steel pipe.

Above: The sleeping area of the bedroom plays out the home's gridded rhythm. The screen, which is repeated in the same spot one floor below, admits light from the big picture window beyond. The only noticeable break in the simple symmetry is two metal end tables that appear identical at first glance.

Above: To create a year-round guest house complete with a sleeping loft, bathroom, and kitchenette, new owners renovated a one-car garage. The sleeping loft is open on either side to the main room below, which houses the bathroom and minikitchen. The all-white color scheme was selected as a simple backdrop—the owners rely on guests, food, and sparse furnishings to fill the tiny space with color and texture. **Right:** Popping up the roof along the centerline brings in considerable light and extends the headroom in the sleeping loft. Permanently attached lamps provide reading light as well as supplemental lighting for the living space. Clerestory windows are operable to control ventilation.

Far left: THIS THREE-STORY APARTMENT DEFINES QUINTES-SENTIAL LOFT-STYLE LIVING. THE ARCHITECT REFINISHED ALL OF THE SURFACES, SAVE THOSE OF THE ORIGINAL OVERHEAD STEEL BEAMS, AND CREATED A CYLINDER TO PUNCTUATE THE LONG WALL AND ANCHOR NEW SPACE ABOVE AND BEHIND.

Left, top: A BED IS TUCKED WARMLY BEHIND THE CURVED WALL. SELECT WOOD BEAMS WERE STAINED BLACK TO SIMULATE METAL. **Left, bottom:** FROM HIS CIRCULAR MEZZANINE WORKSPACE, THE ARCHITECT ENJOYS A SWEEPING VIEW OF THE LIVING ROOM BELOW. A SWIRLING, SPIRALING RAG-ROLLED FINISH ACCENTU-ATES THE CURVED TOWER.

Far left: The basic principles of solar design and the vernacular architecture of tropical Bali come together in this Indonesian bedroom. The partially uncovered ceiling acts like a sieve, allowing warm air to escape while also shading the room from intense direct sunlight. At night, stone floor tiles release stored heat to warm the cool air. The hand-crafted bed is mahogany, chosen for its natural resistance to termites. **Left:** A curtain separates the sleeping area from the adjacent bathroom. Bamboo mats and an antique painted wood vanity capture the regional style.

Above: THREE DISTINCT RUGS ADORN THE HARDWOOD FLOORS OF A GENTLEMAN'S NINETEENTH-CENTURY

AMERICAN EMPIRE BEDROOM. AN AUTHENTIC NAPOLEONIC CAMPAIGN DESK STANDS IN THE CORNER,

AND CHINOISERIE FABRIC COVERS THE BED. RICH JEWEL TONES SEPARATE THE ROOM INTO AREAS OF WARMTH

AND PRIVACY. **Right:** BEDS WERE ONCE VALUABLE FAMILY POSSESSIONS; AS EARLY AS THE FOURTEENTH

CENTURY, THEY WERE BEQUEATHED IN WILLS. THIS HEIRLOOM BED, EVOCATIVE OF THE FRENCH EMPIRE STYLE, IS

THE CENTERPIECE OF A TRADITION-LADEN MASTER BEDROOM IN A MEXICAN HACIENDA. THE BED'S LIGHT

AND FANCIFUL FRAME VISUALLY BALANCES THE ROOM'S OTHERWISE HEAVY FURNISHINGS.

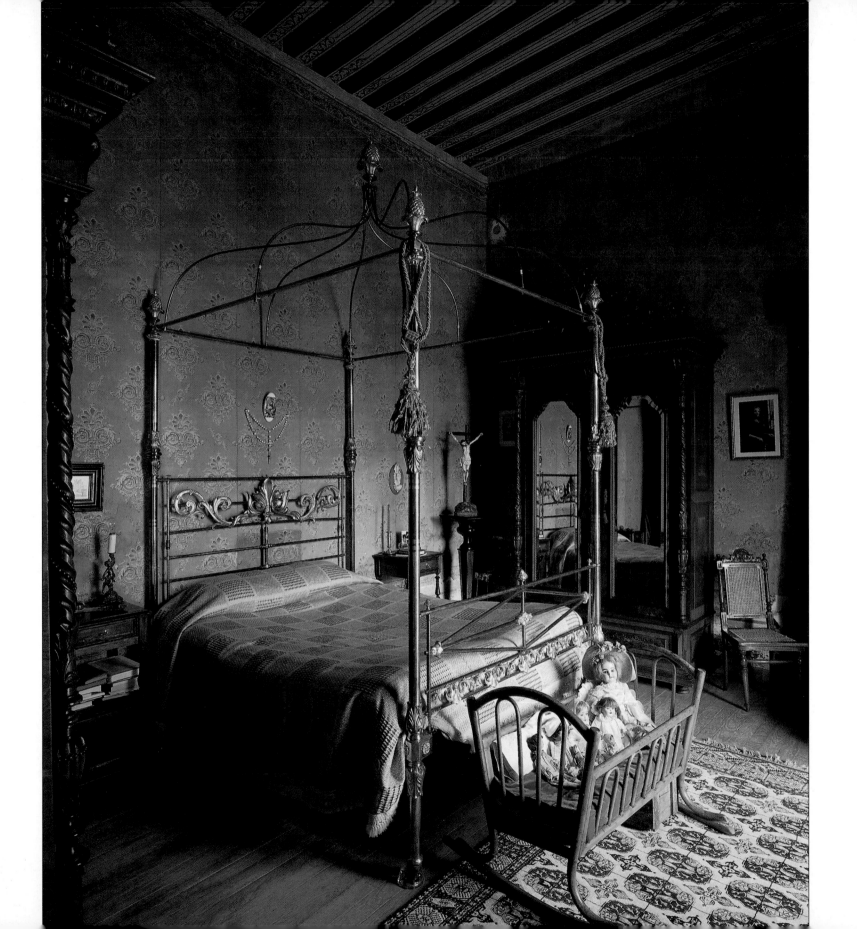

Part Two: Personal Touches

Bedrooms are extremely functional spaces. At the very least, they are a starting and stopping point for each day. For some, the bedroom is more. It may double as a dressing room, a home office, a library on a lazy Sunday morning, or an all-night private movie theater. For others, the bedroom might be a welcome respite to a hard day's work or a lovingly arranged homage to one's heritage and treasured family possessions. And then there are the many intangible functions of the bedroom: the sweet anticipation of a passionate encounter or the memorable magic of a childhood bedtime story.

Historically, too, bedrooms served more than their most obvious function. King Louis XIV actually conducted affairs of state from the bed in one of his many majestically appointed bedrooms (it's rumored he owned more than four hundred beds). Most great houses of the seventeenth century featured mourning chambers, bedrooms designed and decorated exclusively for receiving condolences upon the death of a loved one. Aristocratic widows and widowers reclined in beds draped with black curtains and covered in black silk sheets while friends and family paid their respects.

For both its noticeable and its subtle intent, bedroom decor requires care and contemplation. Equate designing and furnishing a bedroom with painting a self-portrait; because it is such a private room, its decoration affords an opportunity to indulge many design cravings. The following photographs offer a glimpse of some of the various furnishings and finishing touches that make the bedroom a truly personal space — and much more than simply a room with a bed.

Left: Sheer white curtains billow like sails on a bed floating effortlessly atop a sand-colored straw raft. Iron and brass tubing frames enjoyed considerable popularity with mid-nineteenth-century bed designers and remain a favorite today with true romantics.

Above: Sheer, delicately patterned curtains and a gathered dust ruffle soften the metal frame of this French camp bed. Matching the scalloped coverlet to the wallpaper keeps the room invitingly simple and relaxing.

Above: THIS SMALL GUEST ROOM WAS DESIGNED AROUND A WONDERFUL EIGHTEENTH-CENTURY PRINTED FOOTBOARD DISCOVERED BY ACCIDENT AT AN AUCTION. THE BED RAILS, HEADBOARD, AND WALL PANELING WERE NEWLY CONSTRUCTED AND FINISHED TO COMPLEMENT THE RARE FIND. EQUALLY UNUSUAL IS THE TWO-TIERED FRENCH SIDE TABLE, CIRCA 1930, WHICH WAS CARVED FROM ONE PIECE OF WOOD. **Right:** THE BEDROOM OF A WORLD TRAVELER AND PASSIONATE COLLECTOR BRINGS TO MIND MEMORIES OF FOREIGN JOURNEYS. THE INTERNATIONAL FURNISHINGS INCLUDE AN ORIGINAL LATE-NINETEENTH-CENTURY PAINTED PORTUGUESE TOLE BED AND LAMPS FEATURING GLAZED ITALIAN POTTERY. THE COLOR SCHEME AND TWO-TONE SILK TAFFETA CORONET CANOPY REFLECT RUSSIAN DESIGN INFLUENCES. THE PLANK FLOOR WAS CAREFULLY STENCILED IN AN ELABORATE PARQUET PATTERN.

Above: BEDROOMS, MORE THAN ANY OTHER ROOM OF THE HOUSE, SHOULD PAMPER THE SOUL. THE SKIRT OF THIS DRESSING TABLE IN A PORTUGUESE BEDROOM IS SEWN FROM A LUXURIOUS ANTIQUE BROCADE FABRIC. THE SAME FABRIC COVERS THE CUSHION OF THE ROOMY BENCH. **Right:** THIS REMARKABLY DETAILED TILE FIREPLACE OCCUPIES A CORNER OF A BEDROOM AT THE HISTORICAL STEDMAN HOUSE IN CALIFORNIA. IT IS DESIGNED AFTER SPANISH TILE FIREPLACES, WHICH WERE ACTUALLY TINY, DECORATED ROOMS WHERE PEOPLE COULD READ OR WORK NEAR THE FIRE'S WARMTH.

Left: A PADDED HEADBOARD UPHOLSTERED IN GLAZED ENGLISH COTTON CHINTZ IS ONE OF THE MANY COZY EMBELLISHMENTS THAT HELPS DISTINGUISH A CIRCA 1900 BEDROOM THAT LACKED ARCHITECTURAL DETAIL. PAINTED LINEN PILLOWS AND LAMPSHADES ADD A TOUCH OF WHIMSY; AN HEIRLOOM QUILT HEIGHTENS THE ECLECTIC LOOK.

Left: A TUFTED UPHOLSTERED BED, HEAVILY LAYERED FABRICS, AND MULTIPLE DECORATIVE FLOURISHES—CARRYOVERS FROM THE EDWARDIAN BOUDOIR—ARE REINTERPRETED HERE WITH CONTEMPORARY LIGHTING FIXTURES AND FABRIC-COVERED SIDE CHAIRS. THE BED FRAME UPHOLSTERY IS SILK COTTON TOILE.

Right: A YOUNG WOMAN MIGHT FIND THESE DREAMY SURROUNDINGS IDEAL FOR ROMANTICIZING ABOUT PRINCE CHARMING OR LIFE'S MANY SECRETS YET TO UNFOLD. A LACE-COVERED SATIN DUVET DRESSES THE EARLY AMERICAN BED; THE AUTHENTIC BUTTERMILK PAINTED BENCH IS OF THE SAME PERIOD. THE CABBAGE ROSE WALLPAPER IS ACTUALLY A NEW TEXTILE—APPLIED TO PAPER— INTENTIONALLY COLORED TO RESEMBLE OLDER FABRICS THAT WERE DIPPED IN TEA FOR A WARM APPEARANCE.

Above: THIS DELICATE BEDSPREAD WAS MADE BY TOPSTITCHING A COLLECTION OF VINTAGE HANDKERCHIEFS ONTO A STURDY SHEET. MOST OF THE HANDKERCHIEFS WERE PURCHASED AT GARAGE SALES AND FLEA MARKETS. TO COMPLETE THE DAINTY ENSEMBLE, THE OCCUPANT SEWED VINTAGE TABLE RUNNERS ONTO PILLOWCASES AND CHOSE A LAYERED EYELET DUST RUFFLE. **Right:** VIBRANT COLOR, ETHNIC PATTERNS, AND VARIOUS TEXTURES GIVE THIS MASTER BEDROOM A REFRESHING LOOK THAT IS AT ONCE COUNTRY CALM AND CONTEMPORARY COOL.

Left: FOR AN AVID ADMIRER OF EMPIRE AND REGENCY STYLES, THIS GUEST ROOM WITH ITS FAUX-GRAINED NINETEENTH-CENTURY SLEIGH BED AND HERALDIC FABRICS IS PARADISE. A FRENCH EMPIRE DRESSING MIRROR FILLS THE CORNER AND REFLECTS AN ANTIQUE CHINESE CABINET. A WOVEN DAMASK IMPROVISES AS A HEADBOARD. DIFFERENT WINDOW TREATMENTS CHANGE THE ROOM'S ARCHITECTURAL DETAILS WITHOUT SEEMING OFF-BALANCE. THE WALLS ARE FINISHED WITH ALUMINUM LEAF SQUARES TO ACCENT THE SILVERY SUNBURSTS.

Above: IN TUDOR ENGLAND, HEADBOARDS WERE INTRICATELY CARVED; MANY DISPLAYED THE OWNER'S COAT OF ARMS. THIS ORNATELY CARVED AND EMBELLISHED HEADBOARD DISPLAYS PORTUGUESE INFLUENCES. **Left:** A FAUX-BAMBOO BED, DRESSING TABLE, AND TROLLEY LEND A STATELY POLYNESIAN ELEGANCE TO THIS BEDROOM.

Left: A CUSTOM-QUILTED SATEEN COTTON BEDSPREAD AND COORDINATED WALL PAINT TURNED THIS FORMERLY AUSTERE, INTENSELY BRIGHT ROOM INTO A WARM, REVERENT RETREAT. THE BEDSPREAD IS ADORNED WITH GREEN VELVET ROPE TRIM AND GOLD-EMBROIDERED SEALS FROM A ROMAN SHOP KNOWN FOR ITS PAPAL ROBES. A BUILT-IN WALL NICHE ALLOWS THE SPANISH SAINT OF GOOD EYESIGHT TO WATCH OVER THE OCCUPANTS, ONE OF WHOM SUFFERS FROM FAILING VISION. **Above:** SEVERAL LAYERS OF RANDOMLY APPLIED WATER-BASED PAINTS CONTRIBUTE TO THE DRAMATIC, HAUNTING LOOK OF THIS DEEP RED BEDROOM. ADDING TO THE OLD WORLD THEATRICAL ALLURE ARE A TAPESTRY-STYLE BEDSPREAD, RUBY RED FULL-LENGTH CURTAINS, AND A FLOATING HEADBOARD, WHICH IS A WROUGHT-IRON GRILLE HUNG DIRECTLY ON THE WALL RATHER THAN ATTACHED TO THE BED FRAME.

Above, left: FOR URBAN DWELLERS LIVING IN ONE ROOM OR SIMILARLY COMPACT QUARTERS, BEDROOMS ARE OFTEN SEEN ONLY AT NIGHT, WHEN A MULTIPURPOSE ROOM IS CONVERTED INTO A SLEEPING SPACE WITH THE TOSS OF A BLANKET. BY DAY, THIS IMPERIAL-STYLE, SILK-UPHOLSTERED MATTRESS IS AN ELEGANT, ANTIQUE-LOOKING COUCH. **Above, right:** GRAY, BLUE, CREAM, AND TAUPE CERAMIC TILES PROVIDE A COLORFUL SPRINGBOARD FOR THE MONOCHROMATIC FURNISHINGS AND WALLS FAUX-FINISHED TO RESEMBLE PARCHMENT. OTHER UTILITARIAN OBJECTS TAKE ON ARTISTIC STATURE: OLD-FASHIONED HAND-HELD LIBRARY LAMPS PROVIDE PORTABLE TASK LIGHTING AND THE ONLY CHAIR IN THE ROOM IS DRAMATICALLY DRAPED WITH A WOOL PILE SLIPCOVER. **Right:** SPARE BEDROOMS ARE HARD TO COME BY. THIS ROOM OCCUPIES AN AWKWARD SPACE ON THE TOP FLOOR OF A MULTISTORY SEASIDE HOME. TO BALANCE THE UNUSUAL VERTICAL ELEMENTS, THE DESIGNER ADDED A TROUGH ALONG THE BASEBOARD AND A LOW MID-NINETEENTH-CENTURY-AMERICAN CAST IRON DAYBED UPHOLSTERED IN GLAZED SILK. THE SAND PIT—A BOLD USE OF FLOOR SPACE—AND LACQUERED RICE PAPER USED TO ADD TEXTURE TO THE FLOORING GIVE THE ROOM AN ETHEREAL QUALITY. THE BIRD CAGE IS AN AUTHENTIC EIGHTEENTH-CENTURY IRON SCROLL DESIGN.

Above: A GUATEMALAN CANVAS WALL HANGING, ORIGINALLY PAINTED AS A BACKDROP FOR A MEXICAN STREET PHOTOGRAPHER, TRANSPORTS A LOS ANGELES BEDROOM SOUTH OF THE BORDER. THE HANDMADE, ONE-OF-A-KIND NIGHTSTANDS FEATURE HAMMERED-TIN-CAN DRAWER FRONTS, GIVING THE ROOM A DECIDEDLY ETHNIC FLAIR. **Left:** A TROPICAL COLOR SCHEME AND GOLD-LEAF PALM TREE CAST AN INVITING LATIN RHYTHM OVER THIS LONDON BEDROOM. A RUG FROM OAXACA, MEXICO, AND ORIGINAL ARTWORK BY THE OCCUPANT'S FRIENDS DECORATE THE TRANSPLANTED PARADISE.

Right, above: THIS EIGHTEENTH-CENTURY GUSTAVIAN-STYLE SWEDISH BED RECEIVED A SPECIAL PAINT TREATMENT TO SIMULATE AN AGED FINISH; THE DESIGNER FIRST APPLIED A WHITEWASH OVER BLUE BASE PAINT AND THEN TREATED BOTH WITH A COMPOUND FORMULATED TO MAKE THE PAINT SHRINK AND CRACKLE. A QUAINT TOILE DE JOUY COTTAGE PRINT ENVELOPS THE HIDEAWAY. **Right, below:** WRAPAROUND PINE CABINETRY CUSTOM-DESIGNED BY BEVERLY ELLSLEY TRANSFORMS AN ORDINARY CORNER INTO A PRIVATE READING ROOM. THE CAPTIVATING WINDOW TREATMENT IS ACTUALLY A HAND-PAINTED SHADE. **Far right:** VIBRANT-COLORED SHEETS PROVIDE A STARK CONTRAST TO THE CENTURY-OLD WOODWORK FRAMING A SLEEPING ALCOVE IN AN IRISH ESTATE HOME.

Sources

Architects and Interior Designers

Page 6
Peter Moore & Associates
New York, NY
(212) 861-5544

Page 9
JS Brown Design
Corona del Mar, CA
(714) 474-9233

Pages 10, 12, and 29
Hutton Wilkinson, Inc.
Los Angeles, CA
(213) 874-7760

Page 11
Llanarte/Lemeau & Llana
New York, NY
(212) 675-5190

Page 13
David Barrett, FASID
New York, NY
(212) 688-0950

Page 14
Mark Mack Architect
San Francisco, CA
(415) 777-5305
Santa Monica, CA
(310) 822-0094

Page 15
Frank Gehry and Associates
Santa Monica, CA
(310) 828-6088

Page 16
Roberto Redo
Eldorado 2000
Mexico City, Mexico

Page 17, top
Charles Riley Designer
New York, NY
(212) 473-4173
Los Angeles
(213) 383-5838

Page 17, bottom
Ron Wagner/Timothy
    Vandamne
Ron Wagner Design
New York, NY
(212) 674-3070

Page 18
Barbara Barry, Inc.
Los Angeles, CA
(310) 276-9977

Page 19
Jarrett Hedborg
Studio City, CA
(818) 501-4239

Page 21, bottom
the late Max Gordon

Page 22 and 23
Steve Arnold
West Hollywood, CA
(310) 657-1029

Page 26
Patricia Crane Associates
Narberth, PA
(215) 668-4770

Page 27, top
Ronnette Riley Architect,
    formerly Riley Henry
    Foster
New York, NY
(212) 594-4015

Page 28
Connie Beale, Inc.
Greenwich, CT
(203) 629-3442

Page 31, left
Nancy Mannucci, ASID, Inc.
New York, NY
(212) 427-9868

Page 31, right
David Webster & Associates
New York, NY
(212) 924-8932

Page 32
Design by Jeri Kelly
Bauhs & Dring
Chicago, IL
(312) 649-9484
Mural by Chuck Nitti
Chicago, IL
(312) 489-7716

Page 33, top
Design by Ann Brown
    Country Curtains
Stockbridge, MA
(413) 243-1474
Mural by Holly Fields
Hartwick, NY
(607) 293-6136

Page 34, top
Marie Paul Pelle
Paris, France
33-01-42962414

Page 34, bottom, and
    page 39
Barton Phelps Architect
Los Angeles, CA
(213) 934-8615

Page 35
Piers Gough
London, England
(071) 253-2523

Page 36, top
Dave Kent
Santa Fe, NM

Page 36, bottom
Cory Buckner, AIA
Malibu, CA
(310) 457-9840

Page 38
Frank Israel
Beverly Hills, CA
(310) 652-8087

Page 40
Levy Design Partners
San Francisco, CA
(415) 777-0561

Page 41
Steele + Associates
Arlington, VA
(804) 344-0066

Page 42-43
Moore Poe Architects
Arlington, VA
(703) 351-9100

Page 44-45
Kiss Cathcart Anders
    Architects PC.
New York, NY
(212) 513-1711

Page 46-47
Nade Wijaya
Bali
(361) 32507

Page 48
J. Rolf Seckinger, Inc.
Miami, FL
(305) 673-1566

Page 50
Helen Cooper Associates
London, England
(071) 740-0711

Page 51
Dan Carithers Design
    Consultant
Atlanta, GA
(404) 355-8661

Page 52, 62
Ron Meyers
Los Angeles, CA
(213) 851-7576

Page 53
Sam Botero Associates
New York, NY
(212) 935-5155

Page 55
The late George Washington
    Smith
The Santa Barbara Historical
    Society
(805) 966-1601

Page 56
Pavarini/Cole Interiors, Inc.
New York, NY
(212) 749-2047

Page 57
Ann LeConey, Inc.
New York, NY
(212) 472-1265

Page 58, top
Peggy Butcher
Ojai, CA
(805) 646-4218

Page 58, bottom
Linda Marder Design
Los Angeles, CA
(310) 855-0635

Page 59
Caron Girard Interiors
Princeton, NJ
(609) 924-1007

Page 60
Kenneth Hockin Interior
    Decorator, Inc.
New York, NY
(212) 308-6261

Page 61, bottom
Mark Hampton
New York, NY
(212) 753-4110

Page 63
Larry Totah Architect
Los Angeles, CA
(213) 467-2927

Page 64
Siskin/Valls, Inc.
New York, NY
(212) 752-3790

Page 65
Carlson Chase Associates
Los Angeles, CA
(213) 969-8423

Page 66
Michael Davis Architect
London, England
(071) 407-6574

Page 67
Jon Bok Furniture Designer
Los Angeles, CA
(213) 660-1544

Page 68, top
Jeffrey Lincoln Interiors, Inc.
Locust Valley, NY
(516) 759-6100

Page 68, bottom
Furniture by Alfred Cochrane
Ireland

Page 69
Beverly Ellsley Collection of
    Handcrafted Cabinets
Westport, CT
(203) 454-0503

PHOTOGRAPHY CREDITS

© Otto Baitz: 27, 44, 45
both

© Daniel Eifert: 56

© Phillip Ennis: 28, 48, 53

© Michael Garland: 9, 36
bottom, 58 top

© Tria Giovan: 17 top, 33
bottom, 69

© David Glomb: 34 bottom,
39

© Mick Hales: 20, 37, 51,
54, 57, 59, 61 both

© Nancy Hill: 26, 60

© image/Dennis Krukowski:
6, 11, 13, 16, 21 top,
24, 27 bottom, 30, 31
both, 33 top, 50, 64
both, 65, 68 both

© Marianne Majerus: 21
bottom

© Colin McRae: 36 top, 40
both

© Randy O'Rourke: 34 top

© Peter Paige: 17 bottom

© Prakosh Patel: 41 both,
42, 43

© Tim Street-Porter: 2, 10,
12, 14, 15, 18, 19, 22,
23, 25, 29, 35, 38, 46,
47, 49, 52, 55, 58
bottom, 62, 63, 66, 67

© Jesse Walker Associates:
32 both

INDEX

Aldaco, Marco, 17

Balcony, **36**, **37**
Bed
  boat, 9
  bunk, **27**
  canopy, **6**, 7, **9**, 12, **13**,
    38, 39, 52, **53**
  carved headboard, **61**
  cast iron daybed, 64, **65**
  children's, **32**
  couch, **16**, 17, **64**
  Early American, 58, **59**
  eighteenth-century, **52**
  Empire-style, 48, **49**
  faux-bamboo, **61**
  floating headboard, **63**
  four-poster, 8, **28**, **30**, 31
  French camp, **51**
  Greek Temple, **10**, 11
  history of, 7–9, 51
  iron/brass, **50**, 51
  laminate finish, **26**, 27
  landscape headboard,
    34
  Louis XVI, 28, **29**
  mahogany, **12**, **46**, 47
  Monterey, 24, **25**
  placement of, 11, 15
  Portuguese tole, 52, **53**
  postmodern, **26**, 27
  size of, 7–8
  sleigh, 9, **34**, **60**, 61
  spool-turned, **24**
  Swedish, **68**
  tatami, **20**, 21
  upholstered headboard, **56**,
    57, **60**, 61

Bedroom design. **See also**
    Color scheme.
  Anglo-Indian, 12, **13**
  artwork in, 34, **35**, **66**, 67
  balcony in, **36**, **37**
  for children, **32**, **33**
  contemporary, **15**, **26**, 27,
    34, **38**, **39**, **41**
  with deck, **36**
  dressing area in, **40**, **41**
  elements of, 11
  Empire-style, **48**, **60**, 61
  ethnic, **66**, **67**
  fantasy, **22**, **23**, **34**
  functional, 11, 51
  glass in, **27**, **38**, **39**
  in loft, **44**, **45**
  media center, **26**, 27
  minimal, **20**, 21
  Moorish, **28**
  Oriental, **21**
  period, **31**, **52**
  Shaker, **30**, 31
  sleeping loft, **42**, **43**
  storage in, **27**, **40**
  tropical, 18, **19**, **46**, **47**,
    61
  urban, **11**, **26**, **27**, **44**,
    45, **64**
  Western, **24**, **25**
Bedspread, **31**, **58**, **62**, **63**
Boat bed, 9
Bunk bed, **27**

Canopy, **6**, 7, **9**, 12, **13**, **16**,
    17, **38**, 39, 52, **53**
Ceiling
  beamed, 36, **37**, **44**, **45**

exposed, **15**
  landscape painting on, **34**
  oriented strand board, **39**
  silver leaf paper on, 12, **13**
Child's bedroom, **32**, **33**
Color scheme
  blue, **16**, **17**
  monochromatic, **18**, **64**
  pastel, **14**, 15
  red, **10**, 11, **22**, **63**
  tropical, **66**, 67
  white, **42**
Coverlet, **31**, **51**

Dust ruffle, **51**, **58**
Duvet, 58, **59**

Empire style, 9, **48**, **49**, **60**,
    61

Fabric
  brocade, **54**
  Chinoiserie, **48**
  chintz, **12**, **57**
  damask, **17**, **28**, **60**, 61
  French Provincial, 28, **29**
  Hawaiian, 18, **19**
  heraldic, **60**, 61
  Indian *ikat*, 12, **13**
  taffeta, 52, **53**
  toile, **56**, 57
Feng Shui, 11
Fireplace, **39**, 54, **55**
Floor covering, **21**, **47**
Floors
  brick, 36, **37**
  lacquered rice paper, 64,
    65

oak, **36**
  oriented strand board, **39**
  stenciled, 52, **53**
  stone tile, **46**, 47
Four-poster bed, 8, **28**, **30**,
    31
Futon, **21**

Jacquard, **31**

Louis XIV (king of France), 51

Murals, **33**

Quilts, **14**, 15, **30**, 31, **57**

Rugs, 28, **29**, **31**, **48**

Shakespeare, William, 8
Sheraton, Thomas, 8
Skylight, **15**, **36**
Sleeping alcove, **68**
Sleeping loft, **42**, **43**
Sleigh bed, 9, **34**, **60**, 61

Trompe l'oeil murals, **33**

Wallpaper
  antique, **11**
  cabbage rose, 58, **59**
  matching, **51**
  moire, 12, **13**
Walls
  curved, **17**, **45**
  faux-finish, **64**
Windows
  Arts and Crafts, **36**
  clerestory, 42, **43**